ELLE FANNING

ACTRESS & MODEL

DENNIS ST. SAUVER

abdobooks.com

Published by Abdo Publishing, a division of ABDO, PO Box 398166, Minneapolis, Minnesota 55439. Copyright © 2019 by Abdo Consulting Group, Inc. International copyrights reserved in all countries. No part of this book may be reproduced in any form without written permission from the publisher. Big Buddy Books™ is a trademark and logo of Abdo Publishing.

Printed in the United States of America, North Mankato, Minnesota.
102018
012019

Cover Photo: Jason Merritt/Getty Images.
Interior Photos: Ana Elisa Fuentes/Getty Images (p. 9); Frazer Harrison/Getty Images (pp. 5, 6, 15, 19); Jamie McCarthy/Getty Images (p. 23); Kevin Winter/Getty Images (pp. 21, 25); Lisa Rose/AP Images (p. 11); Michael Loccisano/Getty Images (p. 13); Rich Polk/Getty Images (p. 17); Theo Wargo/Getty Images (p. 27); Pascal Le Segretain/Getty Images (p. 29).

Coordinating Series Editor: Tamara L. Britton
Contributing Series Editor: Jill M. Roesler
Graphic Design: Jenny Christensen, Cody Laberda

Library of Congress Control Number: 2018948443

Publisher's Cataloging-in-Publication Data

Names: St. Sauver, Dennis, author.
Title: Elle Fanning / by Dennis St. Sauver.
Description: Minneapolis, Minnesota : Abdo Publishing, 2019 | Series: Big buddy pop biographies set 4 | Includes online resources and index.
Identifiers: ISBN 9781532117992 (lib. bdg.) | ISBN 9781532171031 (ebook)
Subjects: LCSH: Fanning, Elle, 1998- --Juvenile literature. | Motion picture actors and actresses--Biography--Juvenile literature. | Fashion models--Biography--Juvenile literature. | Actresses--United States--Biography--Juvenile literature.
Classification: DDC 792.028092 [B]--dc23

CONTENTS

TALENTED ACTRESS 4
SNAPSHOT 5
FAMILY TIES 6
EARLY YEARS 8
RISING STAR 10
SUPERSTAR 14
MALEFICENT 18
FASHION MODEL 22
AWARDS 24
GIVING BACK 26
BUZZ 28
GLOSSARY 30
ONLINE RESOURCES 31
INDEX 32

TALENTED ACTRESS

Mary Elle Fanning is a talented young actress. She goes by the name Elle.

In 2014, she starred in the Disney movie *Maleficent* with Angelina Jolie. Elle's character was Princess Aurora. Fans loved watching her outstanding **performance**!

SNAPSHOT

NAME:
Mary Elle Fanning

BIRTHDAY:
April 9th, 1998

BIRTHPLACE:
Conyers, Georgia

POPULAR MOVIES:
Super 8, We Bought a Zoo, Maleficent, The Boxtrolls

FAMILY TIES

Elle was born in Conyers, Georgia, on April 9, 1998. Her parents are Heather and Steven Fanning. Heather played **professional** tennis. And Steven played minor league baseball.

Elle has an older sister. She is the famous actress Dakota Fanning.

Elle and Dakota *(left)* have appeared on the red carpet together many times.

WHERE IN THE WORLD?

Tennessee
North Carolina
South Carolina
Alabama
Conyers
Georgia
Florida
ATLANTIC OCEAN

EARLY YEARS

Elle began acting at an early age. When she was three years old, she acted in the movie *I Am Sam*. In the movie, she played a younger version of her sister Dakota.

The actress has always been tall for her age. Because of her height, she often played characters much older than she really was.

Elle wanted to be an actress at a young age. She even dressed as famous actress Marilyn Monroe for Halloween.

RISING STAR

Elle was **homeschooled** by her grandmother until she was nine years old. She began fourth grade in a regular school. But she always felt more comfortable on the red carpet than in a classroom.

Even as a young star, Elle has always enjoyed acting. But she is also a talented singer, dancer, and fashion model.

Dakota *(left)* and Elle did not have a lot in common when they were young. But they became closer as they got older.

Throughout her teen years, Elle continued to make movies. In 2011, she starred in a movie with actor Matt Damon called *We Bought a Zoo*. The movie was based on a true story.

DID YOU KNOW?
Elle's favorite actors are Meryl Streep, Jodie Foster, and Marilyn Monroe. Her favorite singer is Beyoncé.

There were a lot of animals on the set of *We Bought a Zoo*. Elle's favorite was a monkey named Crystal.

SUPERSTAR

The young actress has been in more than 20 movies. In 2014, she starred in an **animated** movie called *The Boxtrolls*.

Animated **roles** are much different than real-life acting roles. But Elle enjoys working on **challenging** projects.

On her nineteenth birthday, Elle reached one million followers on Instagram.

In 2008, Elle worked with actor Brad Pitt in the movie *The Curious Case of Benjamin Button*. The movie was **nominated** for an **Academy Award**. After the film, Elle continued to advance in her **career**.

Eight years later, Elle was the voice of Felice in the **animated** film *Leap!* In the movie, Felice dreams of becoming a ballerina.

When Elle gets a new role, she is most excited to know what her character's name will be.

MALEFICENT

Growing up, Elle loved the princess in Disney's *Sleeping Beauty*. When she got the part of Princess Aurora in *Maleficent*, it was her dream come true.

She starred in the 2014 movie with superstar actress Angelina Jolie. Angelina played the wicked witch named Maleficent.

Maleficent is based on the Disney movie *Sleeping Beauty*. The original movie came out in 1959!

Elle was nervous to star in a film with the world-famous actress. But after meeting Angelina, Elle was excited to work with her. *Maleficent* received an **Academy Award nomination** for Best Costume **Design** in 2015.

Maleficent became one of the top films of 2014. It earned more than $700 million in box office sales worldwide!

FASHION MODEL

Elle has always been interested in fashion magazines and shows. In 2016, Elle got to play a model in one of her movies. And she is a model herself.

This superstar attends many **award** shows and special events. So she needs to be wearing the latest fashions.

Elle appeared in the 2018 jewelry campaign for Tiffany & Co.

AWARDS

Elle has been **nominated** for more than 40 **awards**. She has won ten times during her short **career**.

In 2011, Elle won Actress of the Year from the Young Hollywood Awards. Later, she earned the award for Best Vocal Ensemble for her part in *The Boxtrolls*.

DID YOU KNOW?
Elle was nominated for a Best Young Ensemble Award for the movie *Daddy Daycare*. She was only eight years old!

Elle earned a Women Film Critics Circle Award in 2014. She won Best Animated Female for her role as Winnie in *The Boxtrolls*.

GIVING BACK

Elle has spent much of her time off supporting different causes. She supports the REALgirl campaign. This cause helps girls lead positive lives for a better **future**.

She has also supported the Humane Society. She wanted to raise awareness about the dangers that wild horses face.

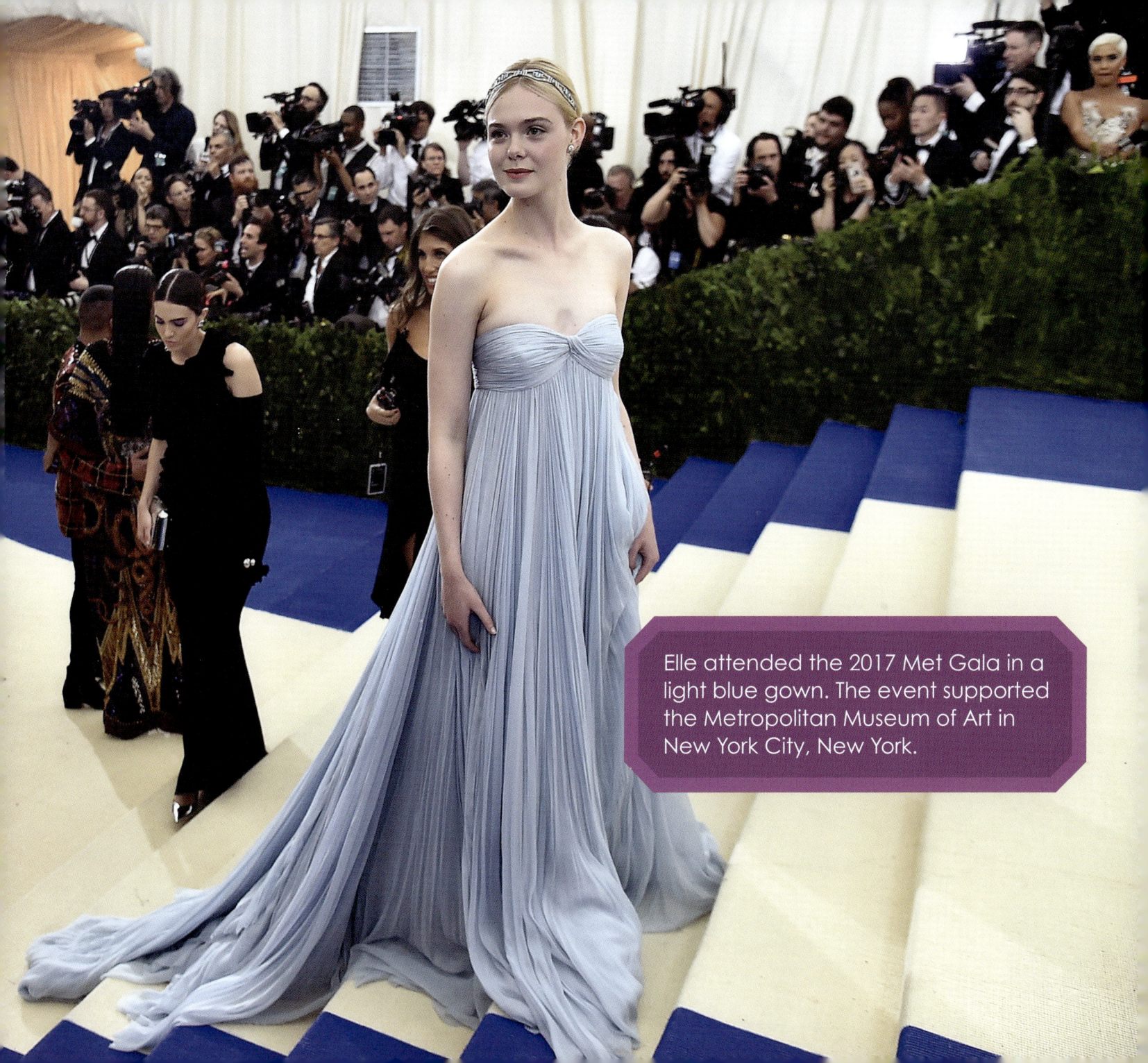

Elle attended the 2017 Met Gala in a light blue gown. The event supported the Metropolitan Museum of Art in New York City, New York.

BUZZ

The young actress and model has a strong **career**. She keeps busy filming different movies. She also appeared on the **runway** for the first time in 2018. Fans are excited to see what she does next!

DID YOU KNOW?
Elle has been featured on magazine covers for *Elle*, *Vogue*, and *Nylon*.

GLOSSARY

Academy Award an award given by the Academy of Motion Picture Arts and Sciences to the best actors and filmmakers of the year.

animated having the appearance of being alive.

award something that is given in recognition of good work or a good act.

career a period of time spent in a certain job.

challenge (CHA-luhnj) something that tests one's strengths or abilities.

design (dih-ZINE) to make a plan.

future (FYOO-chuhr) a time that has not yet occurred.

homeschool to teach school subjects at home.

nominate to name as a possible winner.

perform to do something in front of an audience. A performance is the act of doing something, such as singing or acting, in front of an audience.

professional (pruh-FEHSH-nuhl) working for money rather than only for pleasure.

role a part an actor plays.

runway a raised structure along which models walk in a fashion show.

ONLINE RESOURCES

To learn more about Elle Fanning, visit **abdobooklinks.com**. These links are routinely monitored and updated to provide the most current information available.

INDEX

award shows **22**
awards **16, 20, 24, 25**
Beyoncé **12**
Boxtrolls, The (movie) **5, 14, 24, 25**
charities **26, 27**
Curious Case of Benjamin Button, The (movie) **16**
Daddy Daycare (movie) **24**
Damon, Matt **12**
Disney **4, 18, 19**
Elle (magazine) **28**
family **6, 10**
Fanning, Dakota **6, 8, 11**
Foster, Jodie **12**
Georgia **5, 6**
hobbies **10**
I Am Sam (movie) **8**

Jolie, Angelina **4, 18, 20, 29**
Leap! (movie) **16**
Maleficent (movie) **4, 5, 18, 19, 20, 21**
Maleficent 2 (movie) **29**
Metropolitan Museum of Art **27**
Monroe, Marilyn **9, 12**
New York **27**
Nylon (magazine) **28**
Pitt, Brad **16**
Sleeping Beauty (movie) **18, 19**
social media **15**
Streep, Meryl **12**
Super 8 (movie) **5**
Tiffany & Co. **23**
Vogue (magazine) **28**
We Bought a Zoo (movie) **5, 12, 13**